FEB 2007

HORSEPOWER

HYDROPLANES

by Wendy Strobel Dieker

Reading Consultant:

Barbara J. Fox

Reading Specialist

North Carolina State University

Capstone
press

Mankato, Minnesota

Blazers is published by Capstone Press,
151 Good Counsel Drive, P.O. Box 669, Mankato, Minnesota 56002.
www.capstonepress.com

Library of Congress Cataloging-in-Publication Data
Dieker, Wendy Strobel.
    Hydroplanes / by Wendy Strobel Dieker.
    p. cm.—(Blazers. Horsepower)
    Summary: "Simple text and photographs describe hydroplanes,
their design and uses"—Provided by publisher.
    Includes bibliographical references and index.
    ISBN-13: 978-0-7368-6450-3 (hardcover)
    ISBN-10: 0-7368-6450-4 (hardcover)
    1. Hydroplanes—Juvenile literature. 2. Motorboat racing—
Juvenile literature. I. Title. II. Series.
VM341.D53 2007
623.82'314—dc22   2006001009

Editorial Credits

Sarah L. Schuette, editor; Jason Knudson, set designer;
    Thomas Emery and Patrick D. Dentinger, book designers;
    Jo Miller, photo researcher

Photo Credits

AP/World Wide Photos/Kevin P. Casey, 20
Art Directors/Cliff Webb, 11; Sergio Dorantes, 12–13
Corbis/Neil Rabinowitz, 12 (left), 21
Kathy Wyrwas, cover
Shutterstock/Joe Stone, 13 (right), 25
Unicorn Stock Photos/Jean Higgins, 26; V. E. Horne, 22–23, 28–29
Zuma Press/Daren Fentiman, 5; Jim West, 6, 9, 14; US Presswire/Kevin
    Johnston, 8, 17; Robert Benson, 18–19

1 2 3 4 5 6 11 10 09 08 07 06

TABLE OF CONTENTS

THE GOLD CUP

Four hydroplanes speed past the starting line. Water sprays behind them. The red and green boat leads.

It is first around the turn and makes a roostertail. A yellow boat tries to pass. The boats reach speeds of about 140 miles (225 kilometers) per hour.

BLAZER FACT

A roostertail is the spray of water that a hydroplane makes as it turns in the water.

The yellow boat takes the lead. But then *Miss Al Deeby Dodge* comes from behind. Side by side, the yellow boats speed to the finish. *Miss Al Deeby Dodge* wins the Gold Cup!

BOAT DESIGN

Hydroplane boats are like airplanes on water. They skim on the surface of the water and look like they are flying.

Picklefork hull

Step hull

Hydroplanes have picklefork hulls, step hulls, or V hulls. The hull is a boat's frame. Each hull design helps hydroplanes easily lift out of the water.

BLAZER FACT

Hydroplanes from the 1950s had flat hulls that looked like flying saucers.

V hull

Turbine engine

Two types of engines power hydroplanes. Turbine engines spin propellers under the water. Jet engines burn fuel. The force made from the jet engine pushes the boats forward.

BLAZER FACT

The first hydroplanes used engines from World War II fighter jets.

THUNDERBOATS

The Unlimited class boats are the most popular racing hydroplanes. Helicopter engines power these loud thundering boats.

Sponson

Sponsons on the hull help steady Unlimited hydroplanes. But because hydroplanes reach such high speeds, blowovers still happen.

Unlimited class drivers stay
safe in the cockpit. Cockpits have
canopies just like fighter jets.

Cockpit

HYDROPLANE PARTS

Engine

Cockpit

Hull

SPEED RECORDS

Hydroplanes are built to be fast. They set water speed records on oceans and rivers around the world.

Only a few brave drivers have tried to break the water speed record of around 300 miles (480 kilometers) per hour. But faster hydroplanes are being built every day.

BLAZER FACT

The Spirit of Australia, driven by Ken Warby, holds the current water speed record.

UNLIMITED POWER!

GLOSSARY

hull (HUL)—the frame or body of a boat

propeller (pruh-PEL-ur)—a set of rotating blades that provide the force to move a boat through the water

roostertail (ROO-stur-tayl)—the spray of water created by a hydroplane as it turns

skim (SKIM)—to glide across a surface

sponson (SPAWN-sen)—a piece on the side of a boat that helps keep it steady

READ MORE

Graham, Ian. *Superboats.* Designed for
Success. Chicago: Heinemann, 2003.

Savage, Jeff. *Hydroplane Boats.* Wild Rides!
Mankato, Minn.: Capstone Press, 2004.

INTERNET SITES

FactHound offers a safe, fun way to find Internet sites
related to this book. All of the sites on FactHound have
been researched by our staff.

Here's how:

1. Visit *www.facthound.com*

2. Choose your grade level.

3. Type in this book ID **0736864504** for age-appropriate
   sites. You may also browse subjects by clicking on letters,
   or by clicking on pictures and words.

4. Click on the **Fetch It** button.

FactHound will fetch the best sites for you!

INDEX